Attention to Japanese Food Lovers!

Sweet and Savory Japanese Desserts

By

Heston Brown

Copyright 2020 Heston Brown

All rights reserved. No part of this Book should be reproduced by any means including but not limited to: digital or mechanical copies, printed copies, scanning or photocopying unless approval is given by the Owner of the Book.

Any suggestions, guidelines or ideas in the Book are purely informative and the Author assumes no responsibility for any burden, loss, or damage caused by a misunderstanding of the information contained therein. The Reader assumes any and all risk when following information contained in the Book.

Table of Contents

Introduction 6

Daifuku Matcha Ganache Filled with Strawberry 8

Baked Sweet Potato 11

Wasabi Chocolate Truffles 13

Umeboshi Ice Cream 15

Yuzu Marmalade 17

Apricots Poached in Mirin 19

Japanese Atsuyaki Pancake 22

Matcha Lemon Cake 24

Kabocha Pumpkin Pancake 27

Sweet Sushi 30

Azuki Pudding and Matcha Soy Milk 32

Zenzai 34

Yuzu Matcha Truffles 36

Strawberry Dorayaki with Red Bean Paste 38

Chi Chi Dango 40

Japanese Red Bean Ice Cream 42

Custard Purin 45

Taiyaki 47

Kanten Gelatin 49

Imagawayaki 51

Warabi Mochi 53

Milk Pudding 55

Chia Seed Pudding with Tofu 57

Anmitsu 59

Mizu Yokan 62

Ujikintoki Kakigori 64

Manju 66

Sakura Mochi 68

Mitarashi Kushi Dango 70

Kuzumochi 72

Final Word 74

About the Author 75

Author's Afterthoughts 76

Introduction

Even before Japan had access to sugar, they had already been making desserts for generations. Instead of sugar, they cultivated the natural sweetness of readily available ingredients in their region. Some of these ingredients are mochi and red bean, which, even today, are widely used in modern Japanese desserts.

Making traditional Japanese dessert is also referred to as "wagashi." Wagashi are commonly served together with tea, mostly based on plant ingredients, which makes them delicious but healthy as well.

Many people also consider Wagashi as art because they are prepared with intricate details to mimic flowers and other beautiful eye-catching shapes. This is because Japan has this notion that food presentation will affect the overall taste of the dish, hence making sure that they are plated and designed appealingly.

Today, it is evident that Japanese desserts are now modernized with new twists and techniques. However, despite the modernization, the flavor profile and the attention to details poured on to making them are still intact. This only goes to show that there is an evolution in Japanese desserts.

The unique and intricate flavor profile brought by generations of careful preparation and refinement of Japanese cuisine has made it one of the richest and most delicious cuisines in the world, and it is finally getting the recognition that it deserves.

Daifuku Matcha Ganache Filled with Strawberry

Matcha and strawberries are some of the most iconic ingredients in Japanese Dessert. This easy-to-make recipe is the perfect dessert to serve during tea time.

Preparation time: 3-6 people

Serving size: 1 hour

Ingredients:

- 3.5 oz Shiratamako or rice flour
- 1 oz sugar
- ½ cup of water
- Corn flour (dusting)
- Six stems trimmed off fresh Strawberry

Matcha Ganache:

- 5 oz white chocolate
- 2 tsp matcha powder
- 2 tbsp double cream

Directions:

1. Combine the double cream and white chocolate in a bowl over a saucepan with water. Once the water has reached the boiling point, lower down the heat, and continue combining the double cream and white chocolate until everything is fully melted.

2. In a separate bowl, dissolve the matcha with a small amount of water, then stir the mixture until it thickens, and no lumps are visible.

3. Mix the matcha mixture with the double cream and white chocolate. Set it aside to cool.

4. Once the ganache has cooled down, dip the strawberries into it to coal its whole surface.

5. In a compatible microwave bowl, combine water, sugar, and rice flour. Mix until a smooth consistency is achieved.

6. Microwave the dough mixture for 1 minute. Remove and stir the dough a little then put it back in the microwave for another minute.

7. Cover your work surface with cornflour. Divide the dough mixture into even six portions.

8. Mold the dough into the strawberries. Make sure to cover all its surfaces evenly.

9. Dust with matcha or daifuku powder for an added touch of artistry. Serve and enjoy.

Baked Sweet Potato

Sweet potato is a common versatile Japanese ingredient. It is delicious both as a dessert or a side dish.

Preparation time: 20 minutes

Serving size: 2 people

Ingredients:

- Salt
- 2 sweet potatoes
- 20g milk
- 20g sugar
- 10g margarine or butter
- Egg yolk

1. Pare the skin of the sweet potato and cut it into cubes. Soak in lukewarm water for 3 minutes.

2. Remove the sweet potato from the water and microwave for 3 minutes.

3. Puree the potato and add salt, sugar, margarine, and milk.

4. Shape the potato into ovals like an uncooked sweet potato.

5. Arrange the potato in a baking sheet lined with parchment paper and brush the top with egg yolks.

6. Cook in the cook at 220F for 10 minutes.

7. Remove from the oven and brush with more margarine on top.

8. Serve while it's hot.

Wasabi Chocolate Truffles

Is it even possible to have wasabi in a dessert? Absolutely yes! Think of it as a Japanese version of spicy chocolate truffles. It is the perfect combination of addicting sweet and spicy flavors.

Preparation time: 20 minutes plus chilling time

Serving size: 2-4 people

Ingredients:

- 1-2 tsp wasabi paste
- 100g 70% dark chocolate
- 10g butter
- 100ml double cream
- Cocoa powder

Directions:

1. Cut the chocolate into tiny pieces.

2. In a saucepan, warm the milk. Make sure not to bring it into a boil.

3. Add the wasabi, butter, and chocolate into the warm milk. Stir until the chocolate is fully melted and everything is well combined.

4. Set aside in the fridge to chill for 1 hour.

5. Using a cookie scoop, mold the chocolate truffle into equal size balls.

6. Dust the truffles with cocoa powder. Then they are ready to be served.

Umeboshi Ice Cream

Umeboshi is a pickled plum that you usually find in traditional Japanese Bento. They have a sour umami flavor that will complement well with rich and creamy ice cream.

Preparation time: 30 minutes plus freezing time

Serving size: 2-3 people

Ingredients:

- 4 tbsp honey
- 200 ml plain yogurt
- 200 ml double cream
- Two pieces of umeboshi
- Mint leaves

Directions:

1. Using a hand mixer, whip the double cream until soft peaks appear.

2. Gently fold in the honey and yogurt with the double cream.

3. Remove the seed of the umeboshi and finely chop its meat. Make sure to remove all its pits. Add the chopped umeboshi into the double cream mixture.

4. Transfer the mixture in a freezer-safe container and freeze for 4-6 hours.

5. Stir the mixture every 30 minutes while freezing it.

6. Scoop and garnish with mint leaves on top.

7. Enjoy.

Yuzu Marmalade

Yuzu has a unique fragrance and tart citrus flavor. Turning it into a marmalade is a labor of love, but the result is unlike any other.

Preparation time: 1 hour

Serving size: 3-4 people

Ingredients:

- 300 ml of water
- 100g sugar jam
- Six whole yuzu fruit

Directions:

1. Rinse the Yuzu under running water for a minute. Remove its wax layer by rubbing salt on its skin. Rewash the Yuzu to remove the excess salt.

2. Cut the Yuzu and remove its seed.

3. Peel the surface of the Yuzu.

4. In a large bowl., mash the flesh of the Yuzu extracting all its juices. Transfer the juice in a different container.

5. Cut the yuzu flesh into thin strips.

6. In a saucepan, bring water, sugar, Yuzu flesh, Yuzu peel, Yuzu juice to a boil. Simmer for 30 minutes until the consistency has thickened.

7. Transfer to a jar and set aside to cool.

8. Serve with cakes or bread.

9. Enjoy.

Apricots Poached in Mirin

Mirin is an ingredient that you will find in almost all household kitchens in Japan. It is a type of rice wine that adds sweetness and depth to any kind of dish. Learn how to make a quick and easy dessert out of this favorite seasoning with apricot and cardamom cream.

Preparation time: 30 minutes

Serving size: 2-3 people

Ingredients:

- One cinnamon stick
- 1 star anise
- 3 tbsp sugar (dark brown)
- 120 ml of water
- 120 ml mirin
- Four cloves
- Five ripe and halved apricots

Cardamom cream:

- 1sp ground cardamom
- 3 tbsp icing sugar
- 240 ml double cream
- Edible flowers

Directions:

1. Combine sugar, water, and mirin in a saucepan. Add in the cloves, cinnamon, and star anise and bring the mixture to a boil.

2. Reduce heat to medium and add in the halved apricots. Cook for 15 minutes or until the apricots soften.

3. Once cooked, transfer the apricot in a separate bowl. Bring the poaching liquid back to a boil. Reduce the mixture until it begins to have syrup consistency. Set aside to cool.

4. Whisk together the icing sugar and double cream until the combination creates soft peaks. Add the ground cardamom and whisk again to achieve stiff peaks.

5. Put the whipped cream into a piping bag with a large shaped or plain nozzle.

6. In a dessert plate, put the apricot then drizzle with the syrup from the poaching liquid. Add a generous amount of whipped cream and top with edible flowers.

7. Serve and enjoy.

Japanese Atsuyaki Pancake

Not a fan of the traditional dense and heavy pancakes? This thick yet fluffy pancake might just convert you into a pancake lover after only one bite.

Preparation time: 25 minutes

Serving size: 2-3 people

Ingredients:

- 30g butter (melted)
- 150g plain yogurt
- 450g Japanese pancake mix
- 150 ml of milk
- Three eggs

Toppings:

- Maple syrup
- Butter
- Fresh fruit

Directions:

1. Combine the melted butter, yogurt, milk, and eggs using a hand mixer.

2. Add in the Japanese pancake mix and use the hand mixer again. Avoid over mixing the batter so that it does not turn into a dough.

3. Prepare six circle molds lined with lightly buttered parchment paper.

4. Preheat a pan and put the mold in the center.

5. Pour the pancake mix and cover the pan with a lid.

6. Reduce the heat to low and let the pancake cook for 10 minutes.

7. Put parchment paper on the uncooked side of the pancake and then flip it. Cook for another 5 minutes.

8. Repeat steps 5 to 7 for the rest of the batter.

9. Serve with maple syrup, butter, and fresh fruit toppings.

Matcha Lemon Cake

Put a twist on the classic lemon cake by adding some flavors of matcha. Some tea on tea action for tea time will surely be a game-changer.

Preparation time: 1 hour and 20 minutes

Serving size: 8 people

Ingredients:

Cake:

- 165g golden caster sugar
- 165g unsalted, room temperature butter
- 165g plain flour
- Three large eggs
- One pinch of salt
- 1 ½ tbsp matcha
- 3 ½ tsp baking powder
- Icing sugar

Syrup and candied lemons:

- One thinly sliced, seeds removed from the lemon
- ½ lemon juice
- 100 ml of water
- 80g caster sugar

Directions:

1. In a small pan, gently heat the lemon juice, sugar, and water until the sugar has fully dissolved.

2. Put the sliced lemon in the pan and let it simmer for 40 minutes. Check and stir occasionally.

3. Grease an 8x21 cm loaf tin and preheat an oven to 330 F.

4. While waiting for the lemon to finish simmer, prepare the cake batter. Whisk together the sugar and butter until it's creamy and thick. Add in the eggs one by one.

5. Pass the salt, matcha, baking powder, and flour in a sift.

6. Combine the dry and wet ingredients.

7. Pour the cake batter into the loaf tin and bake for 45 minutes.

8. Remove the lemon slices from your lemon syrup, remove it from heat, and set it aside to cook.

9. Pour the syrup on top of the cake and arrange the lemon slices on top.

10. Divide into eight slices and serve.

Kabocha Pumpkin Pancake

Kabocha is a Japanese variation of pumpkin. It has a sweeter and more moist flesh than the typical western variety, which is why it makes an excellent ingredient for desserts.

Preparation time: 30 minutes

Serving size: 3-4 people

Ingredients:

- 50g butter
- 200 ml of milk
- Two eggs
- 1 tsp cinnamon
- 100g plain flour
- One kabocha pumpkin
- Pinch of salt
- Icing sugar
- 1 tsp Yuzu citrus juice

Directions:

1. Cut the Kabocha in half and remove the seeds. Put it in the microwave for 15 minutes then puree the cooked Kabocha.

2. Pass the flour in a sift, then add a pinch of salt and 1 tsp of cinnamon.

3. In a large mixing bowl, combine the flour mixture with eggs then whisk the ingredients until the consistency is smooth. Slowly add the milk little by little and whisk the mixture again.

4. Gently fold half of your Kabocha in the pancake batter mixture.

5. Melt butter in a frying pan. Pour in the pancake batter mixture.

6. Check if the sides of the pancake are cooked and if bubbles are starting to form. If it does, then it's time to flip the pancake.

7. Do steps 5 and 6 to the remaining pancake batter.

8. Stack the pancakes and drizzle with the rest of the Kabocha on top. Dust with icing sugar for an extra touch.

Sweet Sushi

Nothing represents Japan better than sushi, which is why here's a dessert take of the well-loved dish. It has plenty of tropical twists that will keep you coming back for more.

Preparation time: 45 minutes

Serving size: 3-4 people

Ingredients:

- 70g sugar
- 100ml coconut milk
- 100g mochi rice
- A variety of available tropical fruits.

Directions:

1. Rinse the mochi rice with water. Let it sit aside for 30 minutes.

2. Bring the mochi rice and coconut milk to a boil in a pan on medium heat. Once it has started boiling, reduce the heat to love and let it simmer for 15 minutes.

3. Remove the pan from the heat and set it aside to finish steaming.

4. While waiting for the rice, cut your fruits into bite-size rectangular pieces.

5. Once the rice reaches room temp, you can now shape it into sushi and place the nuts on top.

6. Serve and enjoy!

Azuki Pudding and Matcha Soy Milk

The title might sound like it's a complicated dessert, but that couldn't be farther from the truth. This combination of two much-loved Japanese desserts is quick and easy to make.

Preparation time: 20 minutes plus chilling time

Serving size: 3-4 people

Ingredients:

- 4 tbsp of sweet azuki beans (cooked)
- 2 tbsp matcha powder
- 2 tbsp castor sugar
- 10g gelatin leaves or powder
- 400 ml of soy milk (unsweetened)

Directions:

1. Put the gelatin, sugar, soy milk in a saucepan over low heat. Stir gently. Remove the pan from the heat once the gelatin and sugar have fully melted.

2. In a small bowl, combine 1 tbsp of water with the matcha powder and stir until a paste-like consistency is achieved. Add the matcha paste to the soy milk then blend thoroughly.

3. Prepare four serving bowls and put one 1tbsp of Azuki beans in each one. Pour the matcha mixture on top.

4. Place in the fridge to chill for 1 hour

5. Sprinkle with chocolate flakes and matcha powder, then serve immediately.

Zenzai

Zenzai is a warm Red Bean Soup with sticky mochi typically eaten during cold winter nights or New Years'. It is a dessert and a portion of comfort food at the same time.

Preparation time: 20 minutes

Serving size: 4-6 people

Ingredients:

- 170g sugar
- 200g beans
- One pinch sea salt
- 4 cups of water
- 4-6 kirimochi pieces

Directions:

1. Rinse the azuki beans with water. Keep rinsing it until the water appears to be clear. Remove the floating seeds.

2. Pressure cook the beans with 4 cups of water for 15 minutes.

3. After 15 minutes, add sugar and add into the pot and select the "sauté" setting and cook the beans again for 5 minutes.

4. Allow the sugar to dissolve and stir the mixture occasionally thoroughly.

5. Taste whether the beans already have your desired sweetness.

6. Transfer the beans into the serving bowl and place 1 kirimochi in each container. If you want your mochi to have toasted parts, you can pop it in the microwave for 3 minutes beforehand.

7. Serve while warm.

Yuzu Matcha Truffles

Pure matcha and chocolate goodness. Indulge yourself with this easy to make a treat that will satisfy all your sweet tooth cravings.

Preparation time: 30 minutes plus chilling time

Serving size: 2 people

Ingredients:

Yuzu white chocolate ganache:

- 1-3 tbsp yuzu juice
- 175g good quality white chocolate
- 100g double cream

Matcha and white chocolate coating:

- 20g matcha powder
- 300g good quality white chocolate

Directions:

1. Boil the double cream on a stovetop.

2. In a separate bowl, chop 175g chocolate into small pieces. Pour the boiled cream over the chopped chocolate and stir them together until the chocolate has fully melted. This will be your ganache.

3. Add one tablespoon of Yuzu at a time to the ganache and mix it into the ganache. Make sure to taste the ganache every time you add in a tablespoon of Yuzu so that the flavor will not be too overpowering.

4. In a shallow dish, spread the ganache and put it in the refrigerator to harden. Once the ganache is firm, mold it into balls using your hands or a spoon.

5. Repeat step 2 on the remaining chocolates.

6. In a separate bowl, dust the surface with matcha powder.

7. Cover the truffle with the melted chocolate and the matcha powder.

8. Refrigerate the truffle again to allow the matcha and chocolate layer to set.

Strawberry Dorayaki with Red Bean Paste

Dorayaki is the equivalent of western pancakes in Japanese desserts. However, rather than having toppings, it usually has a variety of fillings. This particular recipe uses the classic combination of strawberry and red bean paste as Dorayaki fillings.

Preparation time: 30 minutes

Serving size: 2-3 people

Ingredients:

- 100 m of milk
- 1 1/2 tbsp mirin
- 1 1/2 tbsp sugar
- Two medium-size eggs
- 150g pancake mix

Fillings:

- fresh strawberries
- 150g Anko sweet red bean paste

Directions:

1. In a large mixing bowl, combine the mirin, honey, sugar, and egg. Once thoroughly mixed, add the milk slowly and sieved pancake mix.

2. Put a frying pan on medium heat. Once the pan starts smoking, reduce the heat.

3. Pour one ladle full of pancake batter into the pan. Once you notice bubbles forming, flip the pancake to cook the other side. Do the same thing with the rest of the remaining batter.

4. Put the Anko paste on top of one pancake and cover it with another one.

5. Serve with hot chocolate or tea.

6. Enjoy.

Chi Chi Dango

There are plenty of Dango variations, but this one has fun and vibrant colors that kids and young adults will love. It has an addicting chewy texture with the right kind of sweetness that will make it a significant hit on picnics or parties.

Preparation time: 1 hour 10 minutes

Serving size: 6-8 people

Ingredients:

- 1 1/2 cups potato starch
- 1/4 teaspoon red food color
- One can coconut milk
- One teaspoon vanilla extract
- 2 cups of water
- One teaspoon baking powder
- 2 1/2 cups white sugar
- 1 lb. mochiko

Directions:

1. Heat an oven to 350 F. Prepare a 9x13-inch pan and cover its surface with grease.

2. On the greased pan, combine the baking powder, sugar, and rice flour and set it aside.

3. In a separate bowl, combine the red food coloring, coconut milk, vanilla, and water.

4. Cover the greased pan with aluminum foil and bake it in the oven for 1 hour. Remove the pan from the oven and set it aside to cool.

5. Transfer the mochi to a clean surface and dust with potato starch.

6. Cut the freshly cooked mochi into bite-size rectangular pieces using a plastic knife.

7. Serve and enjoy.

Japanese Red Bean Ice Cream

Azuki is genuinely a versatile ingredient. It can be used for main dishes, and it also goes well as a dessert, and this recipe is a testament to that.

Preparation time: 30 minutes plus freezing time

Serving size: 8 people

Ingredients:

- One teaspoon vanilla extract
- 2/3 cup white sugar
- 2/3 cup white sugar
- Four egg yolks
- 1 cup heavy cream
- 1 cup milk
- 3 1/2 cups water
- Two teaspoons lemon juice
- 1/3 cup white sugar
- 1 cup dry adzuki beans

Directions:

1. Boil the water, lemon juice, ⅓ cup of sugar, and azuki bean in a saucepan. Once boiling, reduce the heat and let it simmer for 2 hours or until the beans have softened.

2. Drain the beans of it liquid and discard the skin. Put it in the fridge for 2 hours.

3. In a separate saucepan, combine the cream and milk and bring it to a boil.

4. While waiting for the cream mixture to boil, combine the remaining sugar and egg yolks.

5. Pour a ladle of the hot cream mixture into the sugar and egg yolk mixture and whisk until the consistency is smooth. Put the mixture back to the saucepan and cook on low heat to thicken the mix.

6. Remove the cream from the heat and add the vanilla.

7. Pour the mixture in a freezer-safe container and refrigerate until cold. Transfer the mixture to an ice cream maker and follow its manufacturer's instructions.

8. Scoop and enjoy.

Custard Purin

Custard Purin is similar to a flan or creme caramel. It has a deliciously silky texture with the right kind of creaminess complimented with deep caramel flavors. It is made out of everyday ingredients, and no special equipment is needed so that any home cooks can do this to perfection.

Preparation time: 1 hour

Serving size: 4 people

Ingredients:

- ½ tsp vanilla essence
- 60g sugar
- Three large eggs
- 400ml milk
- Sauce:
- 50 ml of water
- 70g sugar

Directions:

1. For the caramel sauce, dissolve the sugar in water over medium heat in a small saucepan.

2. Cook the mixture until the color has turned golden brown.

3. For the pudding, microwave the milk to warm for 1 minute.

4. Whisk the vanilla essence and sugar to the milk.

5. Pass the milk mixture through a strainer to remove lumps and bumps.

6. Equally, distribute the caramel sauce into four pudding molds and pour in the pudding.

7. Boil 750ml of water in a frying pan and place the pudding mold. Cover it with foil and let it simmer for 5 minutes.

8. Remove the pudding molds from the hot water and let it cool for 15 minutes. Put it in the refrigerator to chill for 1 hour.

9. Flip the mold to remove the pudding.

10. Serve.

Taiyaki

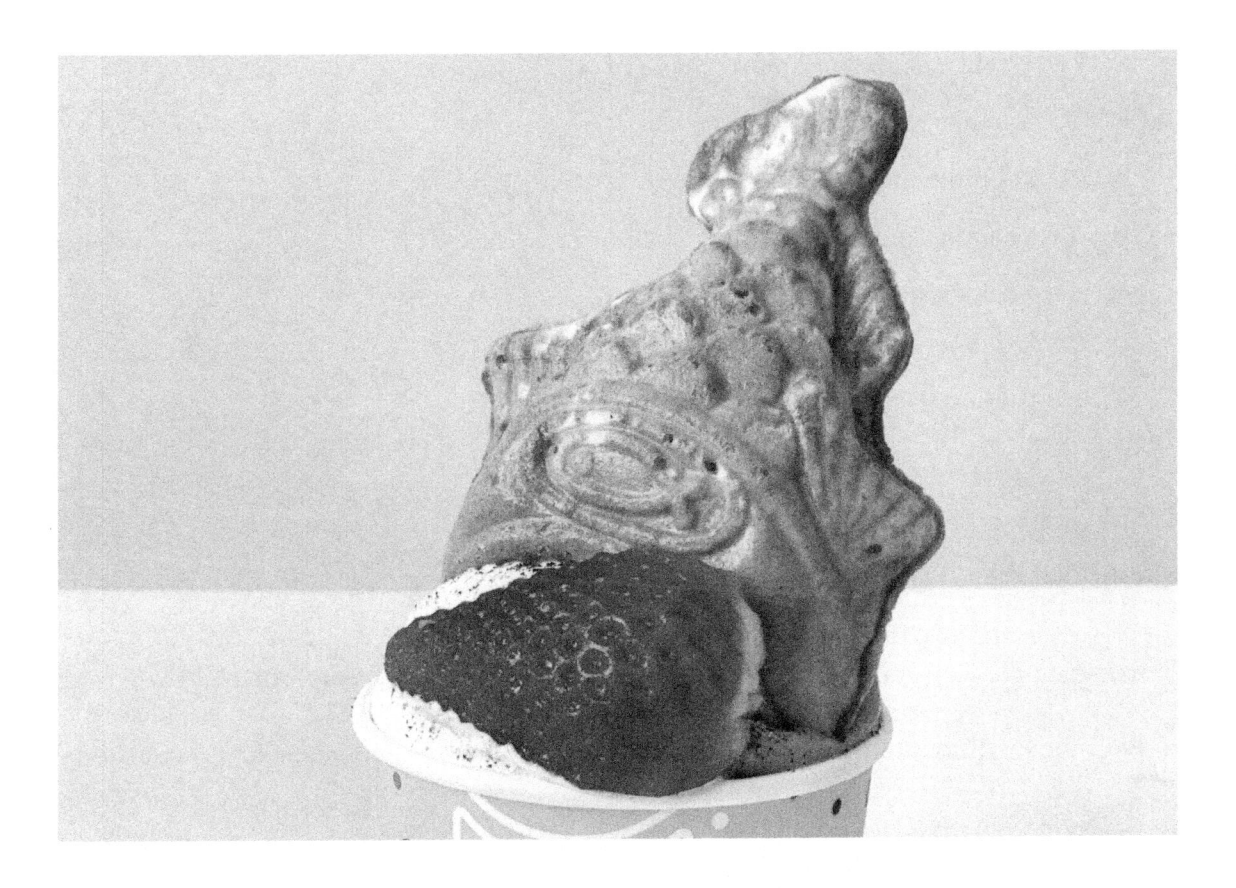

Taiyaki is a fish-shaped Japanese cake commonly served during festivals. They are extra delicious when piping hot, and there are different varieties of fillings. This particular recipe will teach you how to make the classic Taiyaki with red bean paste.

Preparation time: 1 hour 25 mins

Serving size: 5 servings

Ingredients:

- 1 Tbsp neutral-flavored oil (vegetable, canola, etc.)
- 100 g red bean paste (Anko)
- 3 Tbsp sugar
- 200 ml milk one large egg (beaten)
- 1 tsp baking soda
- 1 tsp baking powder
- 150 g cake flour

Directions:

1. Sift all the dry ingredients and combine them in a large bowl.

2. In a separate bowl, combine the milk and egg.

3. Combine the wet and dry ingredients and whisk. Set aside to let the batter settle.

4. Pour the mixture into a preheated Taiyaki pan, which you can purchase in Asian stores or online.

5. Put a generous spoonful red bean paste in the middle of the batter then add more batter to cover the filling.

6. Cover the pan with its lid and cook it for 2 to 3 minutes on each side.

7. Remove the Taiyaki and put it on a cooling rack. Do the same steps on the rest of the remaining batter.

8. Serve immediately.

Kanten Gelatin

Kanten Gelatin might just be your new guilt-free pleasure. It is high-fiber and calorie-free, so it would help you with your sweet cravings if you are on a diet.

Preparation time: 30 minutes plus freezing time

Serving size: 2 people

Ingredients:

- 600ml water
- 4g of Kanten agar agar powder
- Toppings:
- Kuromitsu syrup
- Sugar
- Kinako

Directions:

1. Dissolve the Kanten powder in the water on a saucepan over low heat.

2. Pour the Kanten into a mold. Let it sit in the mold to cool down then transfer it to the fridge for 3 hours to cool down and harden fully.

3. Once the Kanten is already firm, cut it into bite-sized cube pieces.

4. Prepare small serving bowls and assemble the dessert. Put a couple of Kanten cubes then top it with Kuromitsu syrup, sugar, and Kinako.

5. Serve immediately.

Imagawayaki

Imagawayaki is a popular street food dessert in Japan. It typically has red bean paste filling, but the modern version has chocolate, custard, and even matcha filling.

Preparation time: 50 minutes

Serving size: 8 people

Ingredients:

- 1 tbsp neutral-flavored oil
- 2 tbsp honey
- 2 tbsp sugar
- 2 tsp baking powder
- 400g red bean paste
- 240g all-purpose flour
- 300 ml whole milk
- Two large eggs

Direction:

1. In a large bowl, whisk the sugar and egg together. Slowly add the milk and honey while whisking the mixture.

2. Sift all the dry ingredients. Combine the egg mixture with the dry ingredients.

3. Whisk until it starts having a batter-like consistency.

4. Put a pan on low heat to reach 350 F. While waiting for the pan to reach the desired temperature, scop the red bean paste and make eight equal disks.

5. Grease the pan with neutral-flavored oil then pour the batter. Place the red bean disk in the center and cover it with another layer of batter. Cook for 2 minutes

6. Flip the batter using a skewer or spatula. Cook for another 2 minutes.

7. Remove the Imagawaki from the pan and let it cool for 10 minutes.

8. Serve immediately.

Warabi Mochi

Here's another take on mochi as a dessert. This one uses dissolving sugar and Warabi bracken, which is a type of fern. It has a jelly-like consistency with well-balanced sweetness.

Preparation time: 20 minutes

Serving size: 2 people

Ingredients:

- 20g sugar
- 100ml water
- 25g Warabi bracken starch

Toppings:

- Kuromitsu brown sugar syrup
- Kinako soybean flour

Directions:

1. In a medium saucepan, combine the sugar, water, and bracken starch. Bring this mixture to a boil then reduce the heat. Constantly stir for around 3 to 6 minutes or until the mixture has thickened and become translucent.

2. Using a spoon, transfer the mixture into a bowl of cold water to help it set. You could also use a piping bag instead of a spoon if that's what you prefer.

3. Scoop the mochi balls from the water and put them in a dish and refrigerate.

4. When the mochi is firm to the touch, cover it with Kinako then drizzle some Kuromitsu syrup on top.

Milk Pudding

If you are a fan of creamy and silky textures, then you will surely enjoy this Japanese version of milk pudding. It has an almost ice cream-like taste which makes it a perfect dessert during hot summer days.

Preparation time: 7 minutes

Serving size: 4-6 people

Ingredients:

- 1/2 tsp vanilla (optional)
- 2.5 tsp unflavored gelatin powder
- 3 tbsp granulated white sugar
- 50 ml of heavy cream
- 500 ml whole milk

Directions:

1. In a large pan, combine the vanilla, sugar, cream, and milk. Once the mixture is hot, sprinkle the gelatin powder. Constantly stir the mixture until the gelatin has fully dissolved.

2. Transfer the pudding mixture into small containers. Put it in the refrigerator to set for 4-6 hours.

3. Top with some fresh fruit or chocolate syrup then serve.

Chia Seed Pudding with Tofu

A guilt-free dessert that will keep you coming back for more. Enjoy a glass of Chia seed pudding with tofu that is packed with fibers, essential oils, and protein. It is mildly sweet and best served cold. Whoever said that desserts couldn't be healthy has never tasted this.

Preparation time: 20 minutes plus chilling time

Serving size: 2-3 person

Ingredients:

- Fruit slices (optional)
- 3 drops vanilla
- 10g Kanten powder
- 4 tbsp double cream
- 3 tbsp honey
- 50g sweetener or sugar
- 2 tbsp chia seeds
- 1 egg
- 450ml soya milk

Directions:

1. Warm the soya milk with vanilla extract, honey, and double cream. Stir well until all the ingredients are well mixed. Pay attention to the heat and avoid bringing the mixture to a boil.

2. Transfer the mixture to an individual container. Put the container in the fridge to set.

3. Serve with a scoop of cream, a drizzle of honey, and fruit toppings.

4. Enjoy.

Anmitsu

Anmitsu is a warm spring day medley of sweet red bean paste, sweet and tart fruits, and Kantan jelly. It is another example of a guilt-free traditional Japanese Dessert.

Preparation time: 30 mins

Serving size: 4 people

Ingredients:

Kanten Jelly:

- 1 to 2 tablespoons sugar
- One ⅔ cup water
- ½ stick kanten

Syrup:

- Optional: 1 tablespoon lemon juice
- ⅔ cup of sugar
- ¼ cup of water

Serving:

- Fruit of your choice
- ⅓ cup Anko

Directions:

1. For the Kanten jelly, let the Kanten soak in water for 1 hour. Once soft, separate the Kanten from the water. Reserve the water for later. Boil the Kanten and its water until the Kanten fully dissolves. Put sugar and stir until it fully dissolves. Transfer to a clean container and set aside to cool.

2. For the syrup, combine sugar and water in a saucepan over low heat to dissolve the sugar. Mix the lemon juice and remove the pan from heat. Set aside to cool down.

3. Cut the Kanten jelly into bite-size cubes.

4. Prepare a deep bowl and put a layer of Kanten Jelly. Arrange your fruits of choice and put a generous scope of Anko then drizzle with the syrup you made.

5. Serve while cold.

Mizu Yokan

Mizu Yokan is jelly wagashi commonly served during tea time. It is a refreshing dessert commonly served during hot summer months.

Preparation time: 1 hour 15 minutes

Serving size: 4 people

Ingredients:

- 1 ½ cup Anko
- 1 cup brown sugar
- One ¼ cup water
- Water for soaking kanten
- One stick dried kanten

Directions:

1. Put water in a large bowl and soak the Kanten stick for 1 hour or until it has become soft.

2. Separate the solid Kanten pieces from the water and squeeze the excess liquid. Do not throw the water.

3. Heat the Kanten pieces and the water used for soaking in a small saucepan. Stir until the Kanten fully dissolves. Add in sugar and continue stirring.

4. Add the Anko and still continue to stir.

5. Transfer the mixture into a plastic container. Set aside to cool. Once it has reached room temperature, put it in the refrigerator to chill.

6. Cut into rectangular bite-size pieces then serve.

Ujikintoki Kakigori

Ujikintoki Kakigori is a shaved iced dessert with a rich Uji flavor. It is a traditional Japanese dessert commonly served during summer festivals.

Preparation time: 20 minutes

Serving size: 1 serving

Ingredients:

- Ice cubes or a block of ice
- 2 tbsp Anko
- 2 tbsp sweetened condensed milk
- 2 tsp granulated sugar
- 1 tsp green tea powder
- Fruits (Optional)

Directions:

1. Dissolve the granulated sugar and green tea powder with 2 tsp of hot water to make a syrup. Set aside to cool down.

2. Using a shave ice machine, shave the block of ice.

3. Pour the cooled down green tea syrup on top of the freshly shaved iced and mix gently.

4. Put a generous spoonful of Anko and arrange your fruits of choice.

5. Drizzle the sweetened condensed milk on top and then serve immediately.

Manju

Manju is a type of steamed cake filled with sweet red bean. It is like the dessert version of a meat bun that has a soft exterior and juicy filling.

Preparation time: 55 minutes

Serving size: 12 pieces

Ingredients:

- ¾ lb. of Anko
- ⅔ - ¾ cup of water
- ¼ sugar
- 3 tsp baking powder
- 2 ½ cups all-purpose flour

Directions:

1. Run the baking powder and flour in a sift. Combine them with sugar and slowly pour water into the mixture. Stir constantly to mix all the ingredients.

2. Knead the dough until it becomes pliable and smooth.

3. Cut the dough into equal 12 pieces. Shape the dough into balls then flatten them.

4. Place a scoop of Anko in the center of the flattened dough. Cover the filling with excess dough. Repeat the same step with the rest of the remaining dough.

5. Steam the cakes for 10 minutes.

6. Serve while it's hot.

Sakura Mochi

Nothing is a more iconic Japanese dessert than the Sakura Mochi. This dessert is very famous during Girl's day and the entire spring season. It is both dainty and delicious.

Preparation time: 46 mins

Serving size: 6 people

Ingredients:

- 6 pickled sakura leaves
- 3 tbsp Anko
- 1 tbsp sugar
- 1 drop red food coloring
- ¾ cup of water
- ¾ cup Mochigome

Directions:

1. Wash the Mochigome and soak it overnight.

2. Submerge the sakura leaves in water to wash away the salt. Pat it dry with a paper towel.

3. Using your wet hands, roll 6 small balls of Anko.

4. Discard the water from the Michogome. Transfer it to a large bowl.

5. Drop red food coloring into the Michogome according to your preferred color.

6. Put the Michogome in the microwave for 3 minutes. Bring it out and stir then put it back to the microwave for another 3 minutes.

7. Remove the Michogome from the microwave then cover it with a kitchen towel.

8. Put the sugar in the pink rice.

9. Divide the rice into 6 equal portions.

10. Lay the rice on top of clear plastic then put the Anko balls.

11. Twist and tighten the plastic to seal the Anko in the middle.

12. Wrap the Sakura leaves in each ball then serve.

Mitarashi Kushi Dango

Here's another famous traditional Japanese dessert. It is a variation of Dango which are round dumplings on skewers. This particular one has a soy sauce coating which makes it sweet and savory.

Preparation time: 30 minutes

Serving size: 5 people

Ingredients:

Dango:

- ¾ cup hot water
- 2 tbsp sugar
- 1 ⅓ cup Shiratamako or Mochiko
- 1 ⅓ cup joshinko

Directions:

1. In a large bowl, combine the sugar, joshinko, and shiratamako.

2. Slowly pour the hot water over the mixture. Stir and knead until the dough is smooth with "earlobe" like texture.

3. Split the dough into small pieces and roll each piece into a ball. Put the dough in a steamer and cook on high heat for 10-15 minutes.

4. Set the dumplings aside to cool then skewer them on sticks.

5. For the mitarashi sauce, combine the soy sauce, sugar, and water in a saucepan. Bring the mixture to a boil.

6. Add the Katakuriko scratch to the sauce. Remove from heat.

7. Drizzle the sauce on the dumplings.

8. Serve and enjoy.

Kuzumochi

Kudzu is the main ingredient of this dessert. It comes from the root of the Kuzu plant. It is a thick and starchy ingredient, which is why this dessert does not only satisfy your sweet to craving but hunger as well.

Preparation time: 20 minutes

Serving size: 3-4 people

Ingredients:

- 10oz water
- 2oz kudzu
- Anko
- Roasted Soybean flour

Directions:

1. Dissolve the Kudzu with water on a pan over low heat. Bring the mixture to a boil and stir continuously until the mixture thickens.

2. Once the Kudzu starts to become semi-transparent, remove it from the heat and continue stirring until it becomes shiny.

3. Spoon a portion of the Kudzu and put it in a bowl of cold water.

4. Drain the water.

5. Serve with Anko or roasted soybean flour on top.

Final Word

Open your eyes to a whole new variety of desserts with these recipes. Add your own twist and flair to make it fit your palette. You can add and subtract some of the ingredients and steps to meet your preferences.

One of the biggest hurdles you may find when doing some of the recipes in this cookbook is finding the ingredients. You may not typically have matcha, mochi rice, or Yuzu lying around your kitchen. However, with the advent of globalization, these ingredients are much more accessible than you think.

You can buy Japanese ingredients in your local Asian store nearby or have them delivered to your doorstep by ordering online. Buying in bulk is suggested when it comes to essential Japanese ingredients because you can use them for multiple recipes if you feel like cooking any Japanese Dishes.

Japanese dessert dishes are quick and easy to make, so there's no need to be overwhelmed by them. They are packed with natural flavor and little to no sugar, so they are much healthier. Try making some for yourself, and you'd be surprised by what you can do and how delicious it could be.

Enjoy!

About the Author

Heston Brown is an accomplished chef and successful e-book author from Palo Alto California. After studying cooking at The New England Culinary Institute, Heston stopped briefly in Chicago where he was offered head chef at some of the city's most prestigious restaurants. Brown decide that he missed the rolling hills and sunny weather of California and moved back to his home state to open up his own catering company and give private cooking classes.

Heston lives in California with his beautiful wife of 18 years and his two daughters who also have aspirations to follow in their father's footsteps and pursue careers in the culinary arts. Brown is well known for his delicious fish and chicken dishes and teaches these recipes as well as many others to his students.

When Heston gave up his successful chef position in Chicago and moved back to California, a friend suggested he use the internet to share his recipes with the world and so he did! To date, Heston Brown has written over 1000 e-books that contain recipes, cooking tips, business strategies for catering companies and a self-help book he wrote from personal experience.

He claims his wife has been his inspiration throughout many of his endeavours and continues to be his partner in business as well as life. His greatest joy is having all three women in his life in the kitchen with him cooking their favourite meal while his favourite jazz music plays in the background.

Author's Afterthoughts

Thank you to all the readers who invested time and money into my book! I cherish every one of you and hope you took the same pleasure in reading it as I did in writing it.

Out of all of the books out there, you chose mine and for that I am truly grateful. It makes the effort worth it when I know my readers are enjoying my work from beginning to end.

Please take a few minutes to write an Amazon review so that others can benefit from your opinions and insight. Your review will help countless other readers make an informed choice

Thank you so much,

Heston Brown

Printed in Great Britain
by Amazon